RUTHERFORD B. HAYES

OUR NINETEENTH PRESIDENT

by Sandra Francis

THE CHILD'S WORLD®

The Child's World

Published in the United States of America

The Child's World®
1980 Lookout Drive • Mankato, MN 56003-1705
800-599-READ • www.childsworld.com

Acknowledgments
The Child's World®: Mary Berendes, Publishing Director

The Creative Spark: Mary McGavic, Project Director; Shari Joffe, Editorial Director; Deborah Goodsite, Photo Research; Nancy Ratkiewich, Page Production

The Design Lab: Kathleen Petelinsek, Design

Content Adviser: Tom Culbertson, Executive Director, Rutherford B. Hayes Presidential Center, Spiegel Grove, Fremont, Ohio

Photos
Cover and page 3: White House Historical Association (White House Collection) (45), detail; White House Historical Association (White House Collection) (45)

Interior: Alamy: 11 and 38 bottom (North Wind Picture Archives); The Art Archive: 23, 27, 31 (Culver Pictures); Corbis: 19, 25; The Granger Collection, New York: 4 and 39, 5 and 28 top, 18 left, 18 right, 21, 29; The Image Works: 20 (US National Archives/Roger-Viollet), 22 (Topham); iStockphoto: 44 (Tim Fan); North Wind Picture Archives: 34 (North Wind); Rutherford B. Hayes Presidential Center: 7, 8, 9, 10, 13, 15, 16, 26, 32, 35, 37; U.S. Air Force photo: 45; White House Historical Association: 36 (White House Collection) (172), detail.

Library of Congress Cataloging-in-Publication Data
Francis, Sandra.
  Rutherford B. Hayes / by Sandra Francis.
      p. cm.—(Presidents of the U.S.A.)
  Includes bibliographical references and index.
  ISBN 978-1-60253-048-5 (library bound : alk. paper)
  1. Hayes, Rutherford Birchard, 1822–1893—Juvenile literature. 2. Presidents—United States—Biography—Juvenile literature. I. Title.
  E682.F729 2008
  973.8'3092—dc22
  [B]

                              2007042605

Rutherford B. Hayes was
known for his honesty.

TABLE OF CONTENTS

CHAPTER ONE

A DEVOTED FAMILY

Rutherford Birchard Hayes kept a diary of his life from the time he was 12 years old. He wrote in his diary nearly every day until his death at age 70. As a young man, he wrote, "I am determined to acquire a character distinguished for energy, firmness, and **perseverance.**" One of his deepest desires was to be known as an honest man. Rutherford worked to live up to these goals throughout his lifetime.

Rutherford Hayes was a hardworking man who believed in always doing what was right.

Five years before Rutherford was born, his father moved his family from Vermont to the town of Delaware, Ohio. Mrs. Hayes's younger brother, Sardis Birchard, went with them. Mr. Hayes bought a business, rented farmland, and built the first brick house in town.

Life in Ohio was happy and successful for the Hayes family. Then tragedy struck. In July of 1822, Mr. Hayes became seriously ill and died soon after.

Mrs. Hayes and her younger brother were left to care for the family. Sardis Birchard gallantly assumed Mr. Hayes's responsibilities and became the devoted guardian of the Hayes family.

Rutherford was born on October 4, 1822, about three months after his father's death. Sardis was like a father to newborn Rutherford and his brother and sister, Lorenzo and Fanny. With hard work, Sardis Birchard soon became a successful banker. He took good care of the family.

Ruddy, as Rutherford's family called him, was a fragile and sickly child. But his mother and sister were determined to help him get better. Their devotion to Ruddy grew even stronger after tragedy struck the

Rutherford Hayes was born in this house in Delaware, Ohio, in 1822.

Hayes was born at his parent's home in Ohio. The doctor's fee for the delivery was $3.50.

Rutherford Hayes was the valedictorian of his class at Kenyon College.

family again. Lorenzo, who was just nine years old, drowned while ice-skating.

Fanny was now Ruddy's only playmate, but her sense of adventure and her love of poetry made her a good companion. The two children enjoyed playing games outdoors. During the cold Ohio winters, they spent their days reading. Though Ruddy was still too ill to attend school, Mrs. Hayes and Fanny spent many hours teaching him to read and write. They wanted him to be ready for school when he was well. Slowly, Ruddy's health and strength improved.

Love and devotion was a natural thing in the Hayes family. When Ruddy was just five years old, Fanny suffered severely from **dysentery,** a common disease of that time. After being dangerously ill for many weeks, Fanny began to regain her strength. When she was able to sit up, little Ruddy took her for bumpy rides though the garden on the hand sled. Because he was little, it was very difficult for him. Fanny was very grateful for his efforts to cheer her up. It was the beginning of a warm, close relationship that lasted a lifetime.

When Ruddy was finally able to go to school, Uncle Sardis also took an interest in his education. He sent 14-year-old Ruddy to a private school, where Ruddy prepared for college. Again, Ruddy showed his love and devotion to Fanny. In those times, most girls were not offered the benefits of college. Ruddy knew how Fanny longed for an education. He shared all his lessons in Latin and Greek with her. Later, he wrote in his diary, "In these studies she was very successful and used often to wish that she was a boy so she might go with me to college."

Two years later, Ruddy enrolled at Kenyon College in Gambier, Ohio. His teachers and classmates admired him. He was not only an excellent student, but a gentleman as well. He graduated in 1842 at the top of his class.

While Rutherford pursued his education, Fanny met and married William Platt. She and her mother moved to Platt's home in Columbus, Ohio. Rutherford spent a year living with them after he graduated from college. By this time, Rutherford had decided to become a lawyer. His studies included law, German, and French. He also worked in a lawyer's office to gain experience. But Rutherford knew he would have limited opportunities in Columbus. He decided to enroll at Harvard Law School, one of the best schools in the country. In 1845, he received his law degree. He began to work at a law office in Lower Sandusky, Ohio. (Lower Sandusky would soon be renamed Fremont.)

Throughout her life, Fanny Hayes Platt (above) remained extremely close to her brother Rutherford.

Rutherford and Lucy Hayes were a loving couple. This photograph shows them on their wedding day on December 30, 1852.

Rutherford moved to Cincinnati in 1849. There he set up his own law office. He also joined clubs where he met Cincinnati's most powerful men. Fulfilling what he had written in his diary, Rutherford became known for his honesty and skill as a lawyer. He was active in local **politics** and later joined the **Republican Party,** one of the **political parties** of the day.

As his career blossomed, Rutherford began to think of marriage. Back in 1847, he had met a young girl named Lucy Webb. Lucy was only 16 years old at the time, and Rutherford had little interest in her. Years later, he remembered first meeting the "bright, sunnyhearted little girl not quite old enough to fall in love with." But when Lucy was a college student, they met again. He was taken by her beauty and intelligence. "I feel that you will not only be the making of my happiness," he wrote to her, "but also of my fortunes or success in life."

At age 18, Lucy graduated from Wesleyan Female College in Cincinnati. She and Rutherford became engaged and then married at her parents' home in December of 1852. She was 21 years old, and Rutherford was 30. Lucy was a kind and intelligent person who cared about people. Marriage to her had a positive effect on Rutherford's career. One day, he wrote this tribute to Lucy in his diary: "A better wife I never hoped to have."

Lucy and Rutherford had their first child in 1853. They named him Birchard in honor of Rutherford's uncle, Sardis Birchard. On the day of his son's birth, Rutherford wrote the following in his diary: "November 6, 1853—On Friday, the 4th, at 2 P.M., Lucy gave birth to our first child—a son. I hoped . . . that the little one would be a boy. How I love Lucy, the mother of my boy!"

SOPHIA HAYES

Sophia Hayes, Rutherford's mother, helped care for her family using the rent received from a farm she owned. The rent came in the form of crops and fruit raised there. Mrs. Hayes, Fanny, and Ruddy visited the farm three or four times a year.

Sometimes Mrs. Hayes rode a horse to the farm and gave Fanny and Ruddy turns riding with her. Usually they walked to the river, crossed it in a canoe, and finally reached the farm. In spring they had fun watching the sap from the maple trees being made into sugar. Summertime was cherry picking time. The fall was time to watch apples being pressed to make cider. The children also gathered walnuts and hickory nuts for winter snacks. It was an all day outing.

The tenants loved to give gifts to the Hayes children. At Easter time they gave them colored eggshells filled with sugar. Other times they gave the children pet birds, squirrels, or rabbits. Sometimes the children received quail eggs or turtle eggs and other things easily found around the farm.

SLAVERY

Hayes always believed slavery was wrong, although he did not speak out against it as a young man. When he married Lucy Webb, he became much more firmly opposed to it. He even used his skills as a lawyer to defend runaway slaves in court.

Lucy told her husband a story that made him think hard about the evils of slavery. While away on business, her father inherited some slaves. Dr. Webb could not bear the thought of owning another human being. He quickly returned to his home, planning to set the slaves free.

Before he was able to free them, Dr. Webb became very sick and died. Lucy's mother was left with three small children and little money to support them. People said that she could sell the slaves and live comfortably. To this suggestion, Mrs. Webb replied, "Before I will sell a slave, I will take in washing to support my family." Soon after, the slaves were set free.

CHAPTER TWO

THE WAR YEARS

By 1861, eleven Southern states had already seceded from the **Union** to form their own country. They called it the **Confederate** States of America. On April 12, 1861, the Confederate army fired on Union soldiers at Fort Sumter, and the American **Civil War** began.

For many years, the issue of slavery had been tearing the nation apart. More and more people in the northern states were opposed to it. But Southerners refused to give up their slaves. They were sure they could never run their large farms, called plantations, without the free labor the slaves provided.

Rutherford Hayes listened with interest to the disagreements between the North and the South. He believed the South to be wrong and declared, ". . .it's a just and necessary war. . ."

President Lincoln made an urgent request for 75,000 volunteers to join the Union army. Rutherford realized that he could be killed if he joined. Still, he preferred to take a part in the war rather then do nothing to help save the Union and **abolish** slavery. He joined the Burnet Rifles, a group of volunteer soldiers in Cincinnati. In June, the Ohio governor made Hayes a major in the 23rd Ohio Volunteer **Regiment.** Hayes promised to serve in the army for three years, thinking the war would end in just a few months. Unfortunately, this was not to be. Hayes would dedicate himself to winning the war for the next four years.

Although other presidents served in the Civil War, Hayes was the only one who was wounded. He was injured five times during the war. Four horses were shot out from under him.

Rutherford Hayes had a distinguished military career. By the end of the Civil War, he had reached the rank of brevet major general.

Hayes's regiment was first sent to western Virginia. Its job was to protect the Baltimore and Ohio Railroad from **rebel** raids. Army leaders knew that Hayes had been a successful lawyer before the war. In the summer of 1861, Major Hayes was ordered to leave his position and serve as a legal advisor to a Union general. When Hayes returned to his regiment in October, he received a promotion to the rank of lieutenant colonel. A promotion is a rise in rank or importance. The army gave Hayes the promotion to recognize his success.

The following spring, Hayes took command of nine **companies** of soldiers. One day, a much larger and more powerful Confederate force attacked without warning. Hayes displayed great skill and courage. He swiftly moved his troops out of harm's way.

The Union army recognized his skill and leadership. It offered Hayes another promotion to the rank of colonel, but he would have to leave his regiment. Hayes turned down the promotion. He chose to stay with his friends.

On September 14, 1862, Hayes and the 23rd took part in the Battle of South Mountain. There he was severely wounded by a musket ball striking his left arm. According to one report, "Although painfully wounded, he continued to direct the action, until his men insisted on carrying him from the field." Dr. Joe Webb, Lucy's brother, treated the wound and saved the arm from **amputation**.

Dr. Webb arranged for Hayes to be taken by ambulance to Middletown, Maryland, to recover.

This photograph shows Hayes (at center in back) watching as fellow soldiers of the 23rd Ohio Volunteer Regiment engage in a mock duel.

Hayes asked a messenger to send a telegram to Lucy, asking her to come at once. Lucy received the following message from her husband: "I am here, come to me. I shall not lose my arm." Unfortunately, the messenger did not include information about where Lucy could find her husband. Marks on the telegram indicated it had come from Washington, D.C.

Lucy immediately headed east to find her husband. She spent six frantic days hunting for him in the hospitals of Washington and Baltimore. Finally, she found him being cared for in the home of Jacob Rudy in Middletown, Maryland. Once Lucy was sure her husband was doing well, she wanted to help others. She made daily visits to comfort wounded and homesick soldiers.

After his recovery, Colonel Hayes took charge of his old regiment. Orders came for the troops to

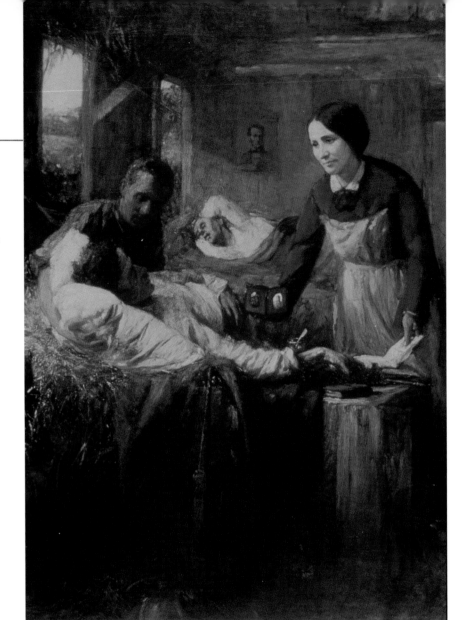

Lucy Hayes did what she could to help the Union army. She visited many camps and hospitals throughout the war to comfort soldiers. She earned the nickname "Mother Lucy" for her kindness.

return to West Virginia. The winter passed quietly. In the spring and summer, Hayes's troops took part in several raids to destroy Confederate supplies. They also helped stop the Southerners from communicating and traveling by railroad. Then Colonel Hayes learned of a Confederate plan to raid Union armies at several points on the other side of the Ohio River. He hired steamboats to carry his troops across the river. They succeeded in stopping raids in several locations. Then the 23rd Regiment returned to its post in Virginia.

Colonel Hayes played an important role in many other battles. In 1864, he took command of troops under General George Crook. He and Crook became close friends. Crook and Hayes shared the qualities of honesty, fairness, and a desire for equality for all. Both commanded their companies of soldiers by setting good examples.

For about two years, Hayes commanded his troops without receiving another promotion. Some of his friends brought this to the attention of General Crook and another officer, General Philip Sheridan. The generals immediately promoted him to the rank of brigadier general. They recognized him for his bravery and effort in several battles. Then General Ulysses S. Grant, the head of the entire Union army, made Hayes a major general "for gallant and distinguished services" during the 1864 battles of Fisher's Hill and Cedar Creek in West Virginia.

Hayes had a narrow escape at the battle of Cedar Creek. He described the incident in his diary on October 1, 1864: "...While galloping rapidly, my fine large black horse was killed instantly, tumbling heels over head and dashing me on the ground violently. Strange to say, I was only a little bruised. . . . I was also hit fairly in the head by a ball which had lost its force in getting (I suppose) through somebody else! It gave me only a slight shock."

The Hayeses named one of their children George Crook Hayes in honor of Rutherford's close army friend. The other Hayes children nicknamed their new brother "the little general."

GOLDEN YEARS

Hayes described his four years in the Union army as "the best years of our lives. Those years were indeed golden." He considered the 10 months he served under the command of General George Crook *(photo on right)* the most "golden" of all. Hayes was a brave and inspiring leader. He gave speeches that encouraged his troops. Crook was a man of action and decision. They made an excellent team. One example of their teamwork was the Battle of Fisher's Hill. General Sheridan planned to attack the enemy head on. But Crook realized that this was a dangerous plan. It might result in too many injuries and deaths among their soldiers. Crook created a plan that was less risky. He asked Hayes to use his fine speaking skills to convince General Sheridan to change his plan. General Sheridan finally agreed, and Crook's plan worked. The Southern troops retreated. As Hayes put it, "They ran like sheep."

Finally, on April 3, 1865, the Union army captured the Confederate capital of Richmond. About 60,000 Union soldiers, led by General William Sherman, destroyed Southern railroads, factories, and plantations. They also destroyed any chance the South had of winning the war. General Robert E. Lee's Army of Northern Virginia surrendered on April 9. Soon other Confederate armies gave up as well, and the Civil War came to an end.

This photograph shows Confederate General Robert E. Lee (seated) just before he surrendered on April 9, 1865. Lee was from Virginia, and he fought for the South. Even so, he truly wanted to save the Union. His leadership and honesty earned him praise from both Southerners and Northerners.

CHAPTER THREE

POLITICAL LIFE

General Hayes was **nominated** as a **candidate** for the U.S. Congress in the fall of 1864. The war was not yet over. "I have other business just now," said Hayes. "Any man who would leave the army at this time . . . ought to be scalped." Even though Hayes refused to **campaign,** he won the election while he was still in the army. After the war, he served in Congress until 1867.

Hayes was a member of Congress during a difficult time in American history. With the Civil War over, there were angry debates in Congress and around the country about how to rebuild the South. Some people weren't sure the South should rejoin the Union at all. This period (from 1865 to 1877) is called **Reconstruction**. Congress wanted the South to be held responsible for the war. It also wanted to uphold the rights of the former slaves.

While Hayes was still in the army, he was elected to the U.S. Congress.

Richmond, Virginia, was the capital of the Confederacy. During the last days of the war, the city's buildings were destroyed in a fire set by Confederate soldiers as they retreated from Union forces. Hayes and other members of Congress were faced with the challenge of how to rebuild southern cities like Richmond.

But the South also desperately needed help. Cities and plantations were in ruins. Homes and crops had been destroyed and thousands of people were starving.

After President Lincoln's **assassination** in April of 1865, Vice President Andrew Johnson took office as president. Johnson was a Southerner, and he wanted to help other white Southerners. He especially wanted to help the common people who had lost so much during the war.

But Johnson seemed to pretend the war had never happened. He wanted to return life in the South to the way it had been before the war. He **pardoned** Confederate leaders, angering Northerners. He also did nothing to help the former slaves, and he supported

Rutherford and Lucy Hayes had eight children. Three of them died in childhood. Before effective medicines were available, children died all too often from diseases for which there were no cures.

Andrew Johnson became president after Abraham Lincoln was assassinated. Johnson's actions during Reconstruction greatly angered Congress —so much so that it attempted to remove him from office.

In elections after the Civil War, the Republican Party ran "bloody shirt" campaigns against the Southern **Democrats**. "Waving the bloody shirt" meant reminding voters that the Democrats had been responsible for the South's secession from the Union. Therefore, they deserved the blame for the bloody civil war. Republicans hoped this would help them win elections.

the "black codes." These rules limited the rights of black Americans. The result was that their lives did not improve, even though slavery had been outlawed. Voters in the North rejected Johnson's plans. Congress decided to control Reconstruction. It sent troops to take charge of Southern capitals. Republican leaders also took over the local Southern governments.

Hayes did not take part in the bitter arguments in Congress about Reconstruction. Instead, he voted in agreement with other members of the Republican Party. Most of them wanted the North to take control of the South. Hayes made no public speeches during this time, and he was not well known to the public. Nevertheless, Ohio Republicans nominated him again in 1866.

RECONSTRUCTION AND
THE CARPETBAGGERS

After the Civil War was over, the Northern states wanted
to keep former Confederate leaders out of U.S. politics.
They also wanted to be sure the South would remain loyal
to the Union. Congress passed the Reconstruction Acts to
make sure Southerners would not cause problems in the
future. These acts allowed the federal government to send
military forces to the South. They also allowed Northerners
to set up and control new Southern governments.

Northerners who traveled to the South during
Reconstruction were called carpetbaggers. They got this name
because many carried their belongings in bags made from
carpeting. Most of these Northerners were educated people,
such as teachers, businessmen, and former soldiers. They
wanted to help restore the schools, farms, and businesses that
were destroyed during the war. Unfortunately, a few dishonest
people went there to make money from the misfortunes of the
Southerners. The greedy actions of these individuals, many of
whom were politicians, gave all the carpetbaggers a bad name.

This time, Hayes campaigned to win the election. He gave speeches about his goals. He said he supported the **amendments** to the **Constitution** that Congress had suggested. One amendment would give full rights to blacks as citizens of the United States. Another would guarantee black men the right to vote. (Women of all races could not vote until 1920.) Hayes also supported the Republican Party's plan to rebuild the war-torn South.

Hayes won the election. But before he could return to Washington, he received the Republican Party nomination to run for governor of Ohio. He decided to accept, and gave up his seat in Congress. In 1867 and again in 1869, Hayes was elected governor of Ohio.

During his two **terms,** he proved to be a good leader. He earned the respect of Ohio's citizens. Governor Hayes took great interest in improving conditions in prisons and in mental hospitals. His interest in the hospitals was a personal one. His beloved sister, Fanny, had suffered from mental illness at the time of her death in 1856.

Hayes ran for Congress again in 1872. He lost this election and decided to retire from politics. He returned to Fremont, the town where he had first practiced law and where his Uncle Sardis lived. A year later, Sardis Birchard died. Hayes inherited the great wealth that his successful uncle had earned over the years. This included his large, beautiful home called Spiegel Grove. Hayes and his family became leading citizens of Fremont.

Hayes was a "pack rat," which means he collected many things that other people might have thrown away. He kept several pieces of damaged china that once belonged to the Lincolns. While living at the White House, Hayes rescued as many pieces as he could before they were thrown away.

The people of Ohio wanted Hayes to return to politics, so his retirement was brief. The Republican Party again nominated him as its candidate for governor in 1875. Later that year, he won the election and became the Ohio governor for a third time.

Hayes's popularity led to his nomination for president in 1876. In the November election, Hayes

First Lady Lucy Hayes received a Siamese cat from Bangkok. It was a gift from U.S. diplomat David B. Sickels. It is believed to have been the first Siamese cat ever shipped to the United States. Siam, as the cat was called, was a favorite pet in the White House. The Hayes family also had two dogs, a goat, and a mockingbird. President Hayes commented that the animals gave ". . .a Robinson Crusoe touch to our mode of life."

When Rutherford served as governor of Ohio, Lucy was a great support to him. She accompanied him on visits to prisons, asylums, and state reform schools, and was a popular first lady of her state.

Hayes's Uncle Sardis left him a beautiful mansion, called Spiegel Grove, in the town of Fremont. This photograph shows Rutherford and Lucy sitting on the home's porch.

ran against a Democrat, Samuel Tilden. At first, it seemed that Tilden had won the election. But some people believed Tilden's supporters had cheated. Votes from three Southern states—Florida, South Carolina, and Louisiana—were in doubt. Democrats from those states claimed that Tilden had won.

Republican voters refused to accept the Democratic victory. They claimed that the votes actually had gone to Hayes and said the Democrats had cheated. No one knew for sure who had really won. It was a very dangerous time in the country. President Grant even sent troops to South Carolina to keep the peace. There were reports that rifle clubs there were threatening blacks if they exercised their right to vote. Grant also alerted troops in Florida and Louisiana. Both Republicans and Democrats sent panels of "reliable witnesses" to make sure the counting of votes was fair.

Government leaders discussed the problem for many weeks. The year ended with no decision about who would become the next president. A special **election commission** had to decide which candidate, Hayes or Tilden, had won.

The Southern Democrats finally agreed to accept Mr. Hayes if he would remove federal troops from the South. Hayes and the Republicans agreed that they would do so. On March 2, 1877, Hayes won the election by only one vote of the election commission.

Samuel Tilden ran against Hayes in the presidential election of 1876. No one knew for sure who had won, so an election commission had to decide who would become president. This political cartoon portrays representatives of the Republican and Democratic parties attempting to convince the country to accept votes for their candidate.

CHAPTER FOUR

A LEADER FOR ALL

Rutherford B. Hayes's term as president started with many leftover problems from the previous administrations. There was the problem of rebuilding the South after the destructive forces of the war. The U.S. money system needed to be returned to the **gold standard.** Many people in the United States needed immediate help, such as Native Americans in the West and the poor people of the South, including freed slaves and Chinese immigrants. These were only a few of the problems facing the new president and the nation.

Hayes was a good president, and historians usually say that he was an honest man. Some call him a "gentleman of politics." Still, his victory over Samuel Tilden created some doubt about his honesty. This often made his presidency difficult.

Because of the problems during the election, Hayes took the oath of office in a private ceremony at the White House. He became the 19th president of the United States on March 4, 1877. William A. Wheeler of New York served as his vice president.

Congress and the political parties usually had more power than the president at this time in U.S.

history. Republican members of Congress expected to control Hayes, just as they had controlled the two presidents before him. Hayes would not let this happen. He gave a speech at his **inauguration** that told people what he believed. "He serves his party best who serves his country best," said Hayes. This meant that he planned to do what was best for the American people. He would do it even if it meant disagreeing with other Republicans.

Hayes was the first president to have a typewriter and a telephone in the White House.

When Hayes became president, Democrats vowed to make his term as difficult as possible. They believed he had won the election unfairly, so they would not help him achieve his goals.

When President Hayes worked to stop corruption at the customs house in New York, he fired two important men. The first was Alonzo B. Cornell, who was later elected the governor of New York. The second was Chester A. Arthur, who became the 21st U.S. president.

Hayes's enemies still believed he had won the election through fraud, or a dishonest act. They even nicknamed him "Rutherfraud." Hayes didn't let his opponents bother him. He believed he deserved to be the president and that he had won the election fairly. Hayes forged ahead, doing what he believed was right for the country. By the end of his term, his honesty, fairness, and independence won respect.

In South Carolina and Louisiana, federal troops were guarding the statehouses to keep the Republican governors in office. President Hayes ordered these troops to be withdrawn. When the troops left, the governments set up by Northerners collapsed. Soon, Southerners had control of their state governments again. The long, bitter Reconstruction was over.

President Hayes is remembered most as the president who ended Reconstruction. But he dealt with many other important issues of the day. For one thing, he tried to stop **corruption** in the government. Corruption is dishonesty, especially when people accomplish a goal by doing something wrong. Politicians often gave important, high-paying government positions to people who shared their ideas and who helped get them elected. These people weren't always the best choice for the jobs. Hayes believed that this was dishonest. He believed that government jobs should not be used to reward people.

To fight this corruption, Hayes ordered that no federal government employee could take part in political activities, such as election campaigns. This angered many members of Congress. Hayes would not listen to their complaints. Whenever he could, he gave government positions to the best-qualified people.

Hayes always did what he thought was right, even if it challenged the views of powerful, wealthy Americans. He believed big businesses often took advantage of their employees. He tried to help poor and working-class Americans. "The vast wealth and power is in the hands of the few," said Hayes. He wanted more Americans to enjoy the nation's good fortune.

Some of President Hayes's ideas were very modern for his time. He took an interest in helping

As president, Hayes worked hard to get rid of corruption in U.S. government. This political cartoon shows a snake, labeled "Grantism," blocking Hayes's path to the White House. Grantism was a common term for the corruption and greed that occurred during the presidency of Ulysses S. Grant, who served just before Hayes.

LIFE IN THE WHITE HOUSE

President and Mrs. Hayes had three of their five children living with them at the White House: Webb, Fanny, and Scott. Webb studied at Cornell University and became his father's secretary.

This picture was taken in the White House conservatory, where plants and flowers were grown. Scott is shown at Lucy's left, and Fanny is to her right. The other child is a friend of the family.

While in the White House, setting a good example for the American people was important to the Hayes family. They started every day by reading a chapter from the Bible. Each member of the family read a verse. Then they all said the Lord's Prayer together. In the evening, they sang hymns and again said their prayers. Each Sunday morning, President and Mrs. Hayes walked to the nearby Foundry Methodist Church to worship.

Many dinner guests expected to enjoy wine with their meals, but the Hayeses never served alcoholic drinks. The president believed the Republican Party should be a good example for the nation. Mrs. Hayes was remembered for this, and years after her death she became known as "Lemonade Lucy."

immigrants, people who came to live in America from other countries. He signed a **bill** that allowed the first women lawyers to appear before the U.S. **Supreme Court,** the most powerful court in the nation. He also was the first president to talk about protecting the environment.

Perhaps most important, Hayes made good decisions about how to manage the government's money. This helped make the nation stronger. Following an idea of President Ulysses S. Grant, Hayes returned the nation's money system to the gold standard. This meant that the government had to have enough gold to back every U.S. dollar that was printed. During the Civil War, the government printed more money than usual to help pay for the war. U.S. dollars were worth less than before because there wasn't enough gold for each dollar. Hayes made sure this policy came to an end.

When Hayes entered office, he promised not to run for a second term as president. Always a man of his word, he kept this promise. By the time his first term was over, Americans respected his leadership. When people asked him to run for another term, he refused. The president told the public that he had no "fondness for political life."

At the conclusion of his term of office, President Hayes made this entry in his diary: "I can say with truth: 'I left this great country prosperous and happy and the party of my choice strong, victorious, and united. In serving the country I served the party.'"

Hayes was the first president to travel to the West Coast during his presidency.

33

For years, Chinese immigrants had traveled to California to find work. They took the most difficult jobs, ones that no one else wanted. When jobs became scarce, other immigrants attacked the Chinese, thinking they were taking all the jobs. Congress tried to solve the problem by stopping the Chinese from coming to America. Hayes believed this was unfair. He worked to limit immigration in a way that was right.

Hayes holds the record for the smallest foot size of any president—size 7.

Hayes retired to his home in Fremont, Ohio. From his front porch, he delivered a short speech about what he thought a retired president should do with his life. "Let him, like every other good American citizen," said Hayes, "be willing and prompt to bear his part in every useful work that will promote the welfare and the happiness of his family, his town, his state, and his country."

Hayes continued to help people. He worked to improve the conditions in prisons. He made sure that soldiers who had fought in the Civil War received the retirement money the government had promised them.

Hayes fought to make sure that every American—including blacks, Native Americans, and immigrants—could have an education. The first off-reservation school for Native Americans was built during Hayes's time in office. It was named the Carlisle Indian Industrial School. Hayes believed that education, private land ownership, and citizenship were key to making a difference.

Rutherford and Lucy Hayes lived out the rest of their lives at Spiegel Grove in Fremont. In 1889, Lucy collapsed while watching a tennis match and soon died. Three and a half years later, shortly after he visited Lucy's grave, Rutherford died on January 17, 1893. He was 70 years old. "I know that I am going where Lucy is," Hayes told his doctor, shortly before he passed away. "I am not unhappy, my life is an exceptionally happy one."

Grim, a "beautiful brindle, mouse-colored" greyhound dog, was a favorite of the Hayes family's many pets. He loved to howl whenever Lucy sang the "Star Spangled Banner."

This photograph of Rutherford Hayes and his children was taken in 1890, after the death of his wife, Lucy.

LUCY WEBB HAYES: FIRST TO BE CALLED THE "FIRST LADY"

Many people don't know much about Lucy Hayes. The
unfortunate nickname "Lemonade Lucy," which Mrs. Hayes
received long after her death, draws attention away from
all the important and caring efforts made by this great First
Lady. Lucy strongly influenced the president to promote many
worthy causes throughout their life together. Early in her life,
she supported equal rights for women. As a young woman
in college, she wrote, "It is acknowledged by most persons
that her (woman's) mind is as strong as a man's. . . . Instead
of being considered the slave of man, she is considered
his equal in all things, and his superior in some." However,
neither Lucy nor Rutherford thought women should vote. They
considered politics to be too dirty for women to be involved in.

Lucy was against slavery and urged her young lawyer
husband to defend them in courts of law. She encouraged
Rutherford to participate in the war to save the Union, and

often visited him in the field camps. Many times, she took her mother and children with her. On her visits, Lucy frequently helped her brother, Dr. Joe Webb, care for the wounded in battlefield hospitals.

As the wife of Congressman Hayes, Lucy's efforts turned to the welfare of children and veterans. During her husband's terms as governor of Ohio, she continued to actively gather funds to build a home for the orphans of Civil War veterans.

While living in the White House, Lucy sponsored a scholarship for Native American students at the Hampton Institute. She visited the school and the National Deaf Mute College often. Her generous gifts and services to the poor made her one of the most loved First Ladies in Washington.

Lucy Hayes (center) and the women who helped her plan social events at the White House

1810–1820	**1830**	**1840**	**1850**	**1860**

1817
Rutherford's parents move from Vermont to Delaware, Ohio. Mr. Hayes buys a business and rents farmland. The family builds the first brick house in town.

1822
Rutherford's father dies in late summer. Rutherford B. Hayes is born on October 4.

1836
Hayes's Uncle Sardis sends him to private school to prepare for college.

1842
Hayes graduates from Kenyon College at the head of his class.

1845
Hayes receives a law degree from Harvard University. He starts his law career in Lower Sandusky, Ohio (later called Fremont).

1847
Hayes meets Lucy Webb.

1849
Hayes moves to Cincinnati and becomes a successful lawyer.

1852
Hayes and Lucy Webb marry in December.

1853
Hayes begins to defend runaway slaves in court. The Hayes's first child, Birchard, is born in November.

1861
The Civil War begins on April 12 when the South fires on Fort Sumter. Hayes joins the 23rd Ohio Volunteer Regiment. His regiment travels to Virginia to protect railroads from rebel attacks. During the summer, he provides legal council to a Union general.

1862
Hayes takes part in the Battle of South Mountain on September 14. He is severely wounded and must be taken to the hospital. Lucy Hayes travels east to care for her husband. She also visits other wounded soldiers, earning devotion and respect from the troops.

1864
Hayes is promoted to brigadier general. General Hayes is nominated to run for Congress. He refuses to leave his military duties to campaign but is still elected by a large majority.

1865

Hayes is promoted to major general. General Robert E. Lee's Army of Northern Virginia surrenders on April 9. Other Confederate armies soon give up as well, and the Civil War comes to an end. Hayes takes his seat in Congress. The period known as Reconstruction begins, during which the nation helps to rebuild the South and accepts it back into the Union.

1866

Hayes is reelected to Congress.

1867

Before Hayes returns to Congress, he is nominated to run for governor of Ohio. He wins the election.

1869

Hayes is elected for a second term as the governor of Ohio.

1872

Hayes runs for Congress again. He loses the election and decides to retire from politics. He and his family return to Fremont, the town where he first practiced law and where his Uncle Sardis lives.

1874

Sardis Birchard dies. Hayes inherits his uncle's wealth and the home he built in Fremont.

1875

Hayes is reelected governor of Ohio.

1876

Governor Hayes is nominated as the Republican Party candidate for the presidency. His opponent, Democrat Samuel Tilden, wins the popular vote. Republicans accuse the Democrats of fraud, so Tilden does not take office. Congress must decide whether Hayes or Tilden will become the president. It selects a special electoral commission to make the decision.

1877

On March 2, the election commission elects Hayes as the 19th U.S. president after he promises Southern Democrats that he will withdraw federal troops from the South. On March 4, he is sworn into office. Hayes removes federal troops from statehouses in Louisiana and South Carolina. This act ends Reconstruction. He also attempts to stop the practice of giving important government jobs to the friends of politicians. He issues an order that stops people with government jobs from taking part in political activities.

1878

Hayes begins to deal with problems in the U.S. monetary system. He returns the nation to the gold standard.

1879

President Hayes continues to fight corruption in the government. He fires future president Chester A. Arthur and future governor of New York Alonzo B. Cornell. In February, President Hayes approves a bill allowing women to practice law before the Supreme Court.

1880

President Hayes refuses to sign a bill that he feels discriminates against Chinese immigrants. Hayes announces that he will not seek a second term.

1881

President Hayes's term of office is over. He retires to his home in Fremont, Ohio, where he continues to help the poor and minorities. He also works to make it possible for all Americans to get an education.

1889

Lucy Hayes suffers a stroke and dies.

1893

Rutherford B. Hayes dies on January 17 at age 70.

abolish (uh-BALL-ish) Abolish means to stop or end something. Northerners wanted to abolish slavery at the time of the Civil War.

amendments (uh-MEND-mentz) Amendments are changes or additions made to the U.S. Constitution or other documents. Hayes supported amendments that helped former slaves.

amputation (am-pu-TAY-shun) An amputation is the surgical removal of a part of the body. The doctor considered amputating General Hayes's badly injured arm.

assassination (uh-sass-ih-NAY-shun) Assassination is the murder of someone, especially a well-known person. Andrew Johnson took office after President Lincoln was assassinated.

bill (BILL) A bill is an idea for a new law that is presented to a group of lawmakers. Hayes refused to sign a bill that was prejudiced against Chinese immigrants.

campaign (kam-PAYN) A campaign is the process of running for an election, including activities such as giving speeches or attending rallies. Hayes won his first election to Congress even though he did not campaign.

candidate (KAN-dih-dayt) A candidate is a person running in an election. The Republican Party nominated Hayes as its presidential candidate in 1876.

carpetbaggers (KAR-pet-bag-erz) Carpetbaggers were Northerners who traveled to the Southern states after the Civil War. Carpetbaggers were often disliked because some came to make money from the misfortunes of Southerners.

civil war (SIV-il WAR) A civil war is a war between opposing groups of citizens within the same country. The American Civil War began after the South seceded from the Union.

companies (KUM-puh-neez) Companies are parts of an army that are commanded by a captain. Hayes took command of nine companies of soldiers in 1862.

Confederate (kun-FED-uh-ret) Confederate refers to the slave states (or the people who lived in those states) that left the Union in 1860 and 1861. The people of the South were called Confederates.

constitution (kon-stih-TOO-shun) A constitution is the set of basic principles that govern a state, country, or society. The U.S. Constitution defines the principles that govern the United States.

corruption (kor-UP-shun) Corruption is when someone engages in dishonest practices. President Hayes tried to remove corruption from the government.

Democrats (DEM-uh-kratz) Democrats are members of the Democratic Party. The Democratic Party is one of the two major political parties in the United States.

dysentery (DISS-un-tayr-ee) Dysentery is a disease in which one's body becomes severely dehydrated. Hayes's sister Fanny had dysentery as a child.

election commission (ee-LEK-shun kuh-MISH-un) The election commission was a group of 10 congressmen and five Supreme Court justices formed to choose the president after problems arose in the election of 1876. The election commission decided that Hayes would be the next president.

federal (FED-ur-ul) Federal means having to do with the central government of the United States, rather than a state or city government. After the Civil War, the United States government sent federal troops to keep control of Southern capitals.

gold standard (GOLD STAN-durd) The gold standard is a money system that gives paper money and coins their value. During Hayes's term, every U.S. dollar was worth a certain amount of gold, and the government had to have enough gold to back every dollar.

inauguration (ih-nawg-yuh-RAY-shun) An inauguration is the ceremony that takes place when a president begins a new term. President Hayes's inauguration was the first to take place at the White House.

inherited (in-HAYR-it-id) If a person inherited something, it was given to him or her when someone else died. Hayes inherited Spiegel Grove from his Uncle Sardis.

nominated (NOM-ih-nayt-id) If a political party nominated someone, they chose him or her to run for a political office. Hayes was nominated as a candidate for the U.S. Congress while he was still in the army.

pardoned (PAR-dund) If a leader pardoned people, he or she excused them for their crimes or misdeeds. President Johnson pardoned many Confederates.

perseverance (pur-seh-VEER-intz) Perseverance means never giving up. Young Rutherford wanted to be known for his perseverance.

political parties (puh-LIT-uh-kul PAR-teez) Political parties are groups of people who share similar ideas about how to run a government. Hayes was a member of the Republican political party.

politics (PAWL-ih-tiks) Politics refers to the actions and practices of the government. Hayes first became active in politics when he lived in Cincinnati.

rebel (REB-ul) A rebel is a person who does not obey the laws of his or her country. The Confederate rebels wanted to leave the Union and form their own country.

Reconstruction (ree-kun-STRUK-shun) Reconstruction was the period in U.S. history after the Civil War. During this time, the Southern states were accepted back into the Union.

regiment (REJ-eh-ment) A regiment is a group of soldiers led by a colonel. In June of 1861, Hayes became a major of the 23rd Ohio Volunteer Regiment.

Republican Party (re-PUB-lih-ken PAR-tee) The Republican Party is one of the two major political parties in the United States. Rutherford Hayes was a member of the Republican Party.

secede (suh-SEED) If a group secedes, it separates from a larger group. The Southern states seceded from the Union in 1860 and 1861 to form their own country.

Supreme Court (suh-PREEM KORT) The Supreme Court is the highest court in the United States, which means it is more powerful than all other American courts. Hayes signed a bill that allowed the first women lawyers to appear before the U.S. Supreme Court.

tenants (TEN-unts) Tenants are people renting property. The tenants paid their rent to Sophia with the crops raised on the farm.

terms (TERMZ) Terms are the length of time politicians can keep their positions by law. A U.S. president's term of office is four years.

union (YOON-yen) A union is the joining together of two people or groups of people, such as states. The Union is another name for the United States.

valedictorian (val-uh-dik-TOR-ee-un) A valedictorian is someone who graduates first in his or her class. Hayes was valedictorian of his class when he graduated from college.

THE UNITED STATES GOVERNMENT

The United States government is divided into three equal branches: the executive, the legislative, and the judicial. This division helps prevent abuses of power because each branch has to answer to the other two. No one branch can become too powerful.

EXECUTIVE BRANCH

PRESIDENT
VICE PRESIDENT
DEPARTMENTS

The job of the executive branch is to enforce the laws. It is headed by the president, who serves as the spokesperson for the United States around the world. The president signs bills into law and appoints important officials such as federal judges. He or she is also the commander in chief of the U.S. military. The president is assisted by the vice president, who takes over if the president dies or cannot carry out the duties of the office.

The executive branch also includes various departments, each focused on a specific topic. They include the Defense Department, the Justice Department, and the Agriculture Department. The department heads, along with other officials such as the vice president, serve as the president's closest advisers, called the cabinet.

LEGISLATIVE BRANCH

CONGRESS
Senate and
House of Representatives

The job of the legislative branch is to make the laws. It consists of Congress, which is divided into two parts: the Senate and the House of Representatives. The Senate has 100 members, and the House of Representatives has 435 members. Each state has two senators. The number of representatives a state has varies depending on the state's population.

Besides making laws, Congress also passes budgets and enacts taxes. In addition, it is responsible for declaring war, maintaining the military, and regulating trade with other countries.

JUDICIAL BRANCH

SUPREME COURT
COURTS OF APPEALS
DISTRICT COURTS

The job of the judicial branch is to interpret the laws. It consists of the nation's federal courts. Trials are held in district courts. During trials, judges must decide what laws mean and how they apply. Courts of appeals review the decisions made in district courts.

The nation's highest court is the Supreme Court. If someone disagrees with a court of appeals ruling, he or she can ask the Supreme Court to review it. The Supreme Court may refuse. The Supreme Court makes sure that decisions and laws do not violate the Constitution.

CHOOSING
THE PRESIDENT

It may seem odd, but American voters don't elect the president directly. Instead, the president is chosen using what is called the Electoral College.

Each state gets as many votes in the Electoral College as its combined total of senators and representatives in Congress. For example, Iowa has two senators and five representatives, so it gets seven electoral votes. Although the District of Columbia does not have any voting members in Congress, it gets three electoral votes. Usually, the candidate who wins the most votes in any given state receives all of that state's electoral votes.

To become president, a candidate must get more than half of the Electoral College votes. There are a total of 538 votes in the Electoral College, so a candidate needs 270 votes to win. If nobody receives 270 Electoral College votes, the House of Representatives chooses the president.

With the Electoral College system, the person who receives the most votes nationwide does not always receive the most electoral votes. This happened most recently in 2000, when Al Gore received half a million more national votes than George W. Bush. Bush became president because he had more Electoral College votes.

THE WHITE HOUSE

The White House is the official home of the president of the United States. It is located at 1600 Pennsylvania Avenue NW in Washington, D.C. In 1792, a contest was held to select the architect who would design the president's home. James Hoban won. Construction took eight years.

The first president, George Washington, never lived in the White House. The second president, John Adams, moved into the house in 1800, though the inside was not yet complete. During the War of 1812, British soldiers burned down much of the White House. It was rebuilt several years later.

The White House was changed through the years. Porches were added, and President Theodore Roosevelt added the West Wing. President William Taft changed the shape of the presidential office, making it into the famous Oval Office. While Harry Truman was president, the old house was discovered to be structurally weak. All the walls were reinforced with steel, and the rooms were rebuilt.

Today, the White House has 132 rooms (including 35 bathrooms), 28 fireplaces, and 3 elevators. It takes 570 gallons of paint to cover the outside of the six-story building. The White House provides the president with many ways to relax. It includes a putting green, a jogging track, a swimming pool, a tennis court, and beautifully landscaped gardens. The White House also has a movie theater, a billiard room, and a one-lane bowling alley.

PRESIDENTIAL PERKS

The job of president of the United States is challenging. It is probably one of the most stressful jobs in the world. Because of this, presidents are paid well, though not nearly as well as the leaders of large corporations. In 2007, the president earned $400,000 a year. Presidents also receive extra benefits that make the demanding job a little more appealing.

★ **Camp David:** In the 1940s, President Franklin D. Roosevelt chose this heavily wooded spot in the mountains of Maryland to be the presidential retreat, where presidents can relax. Even though it is a retreat, world business is conducted there. Most famously, President Jimmy Carter met with Middle Eastern leaders at Camp David in 1978. The result was a peace agreement between Israel and Egypt.

★ *Air Force One:* The president flies on a jet called *Air Force One*. It is a Boeing 747-200B that has been modified to meet the president's needs.

Air Force One is the size of a large home. It is equipped with a dining room, sleeping quarters, a conference room, and office space. It also has two kitchens that can provide food for up to 50 people.

★ **The Secret Service:** While not the most glamorous of the president's perks, the Secret Service is one of the most important. The Secret Service is a group of highly trained agents who protect the president and the president's family.

★ **The Presidential State Car:** The presidential limousine is a stretch Cadillac DTS.

It has been armored to protect the president in case of attack. Inside the plush car are a foldaway desk, an entertainment center, and a communications console.

★ **The Food:** The White House has five chefs who will make any food the president wants. The White House also has an extensive wine collection.

★ **Retirement:** A former president receives a pension, or retirement pay, of just under $180,000 a year. Former presidents also receive Secret Service protection for the rest of their lives.

FACTS

QUALIFICATIONS

To run for president, a candidate must

- ★ be at least 35 years old
- ★ be a citizen who was born in the United States
- ★ have lived in the United States for 14 years

TERM OF OFFICE

A president's term of office is four years.
No president can stay in office for more than two terms.

ELECTION DATE

The presidential election takes place every four years on the first Tuesday of November.

INAUGURATION DATE

Presidents are inaugurated on January 20.

OATH OF OFFICE

I do solemnly swear I will faithfully execute the office of the President of the United States and will to the best of my ability preserve, protect, and defend the Constitution of the United States.

WRITE A LETTER TO THE PRESIDENT

One of the best things about being a U.S. citizen is that Americans get to participate in their government. They can speak out if they feel government leaders aren't doing their jobs. They can also praise leaders who are going the extra mile. Do you have something you'd like the president to do? Should the president worry more about the environment and encourage people to recycle? Should the government spend more money on our schools? You can write a letter to the president to say how you feel!

1600 Pennsylvania Avenue
Washington, D.C. 20500
You can even send an e-mail to: president@whitehouse.gov

BOOKS

Geer, Emily Apt. *First Lady: The Life of Lucy Webb Hayes.* Kent, OH: Kent State University Press, 1984.

Gormley, Beatrice. *First Ladies: Women Who Called the White House Home.* New York: Scholastic, 1997.

Hansen, Joyce. *Bury Me Not in a Land of Slaves: African-Americans in the Time of Reconstruction.* New York: Franklin Watts, 2000.

Levy, Debbie. *Rutherford B. Hayes.* Minneapolis: Lerner Publishing Group, 2007.

Murphy, Jim. *The Boys' War: Confederate and Union Soldiers Talk About the Civil War.* New York: Clarion, 1990.

Nadine, Corinne J., and Rose Blue. *Civil War Ends. Assassination, Reconstruction, and the Aftermath.* Austin, TX: Raintree Steck-Vaughn, 1999.

Santella, Andrew. *Rutherford B. Hayes.* Minneapolis: Compass Point Books, 2004.

Schleichert, Elizabeth. *The Thirteenth Amendment: Ending Slavery.* Springfield, NJ: Enslow Publishers, 1998.

VIDEOS

The American President. DVD, VHS (Alexandria, VA: PBS Home Video, 2000).

The History Channel Presents The President. DVD (New York: A & E Home Video, 2005).

National Geographic's Inside the White House. DVD (Washington, D.C.: National Geographic Video, 2003).

INTERNET SITES

Visit our Web page for lots of links about Rutherford B. Hayes and other U.S. presidents:

http://www.childsworld.com/links

Note to Parents, Teachers, and Librarians: We routinely verify our Web links to make sure they are safe, active sites—so encourage your readers to check them out!

INDEX